Max and Mia

- Poor Max -

Text and illustrations by Anders Rauff-Nielsen

Widowgrove

"Max and Mia – Poor Max"

© 2016 Anders Rauff-Nielsen

ISBN: 978-87-998847-5-9

Published by Widowgrove

www.widowgrove.com

For my daughter Gaia

This is Max
Hi Max

Max went for a walk

Max fell into
a hole
Oh no!

Darn!
Now Max is dead

This is Mia
Hi Mia

Mia went for
a walk
What was that?

Mia saw a hole

Mia saw Max
Oh no!

Let me get you out

Mia took Max
to her home

Let me mend you

I will just sew
him back up

Put a toe
on a foot

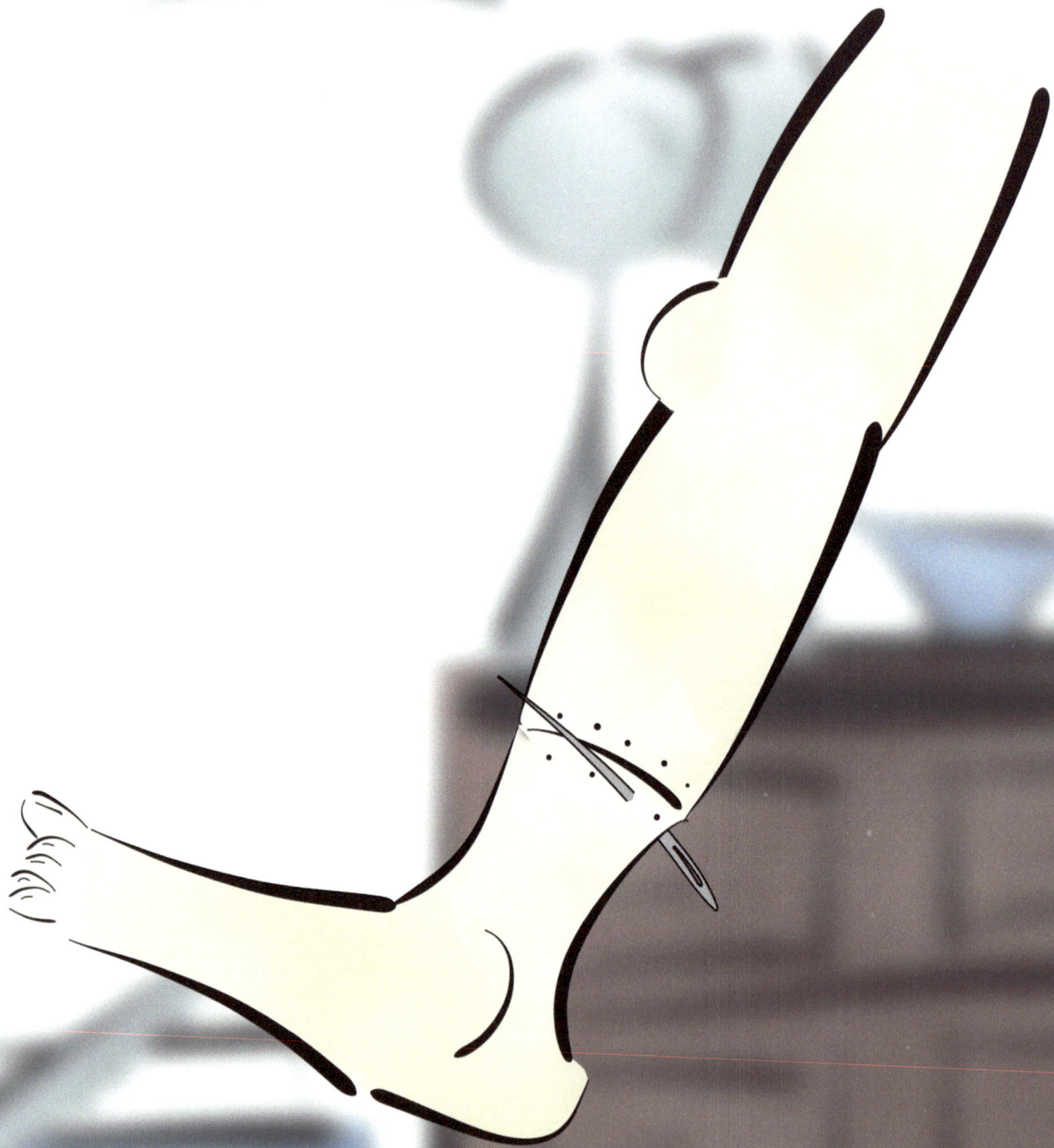

A foot on a leg

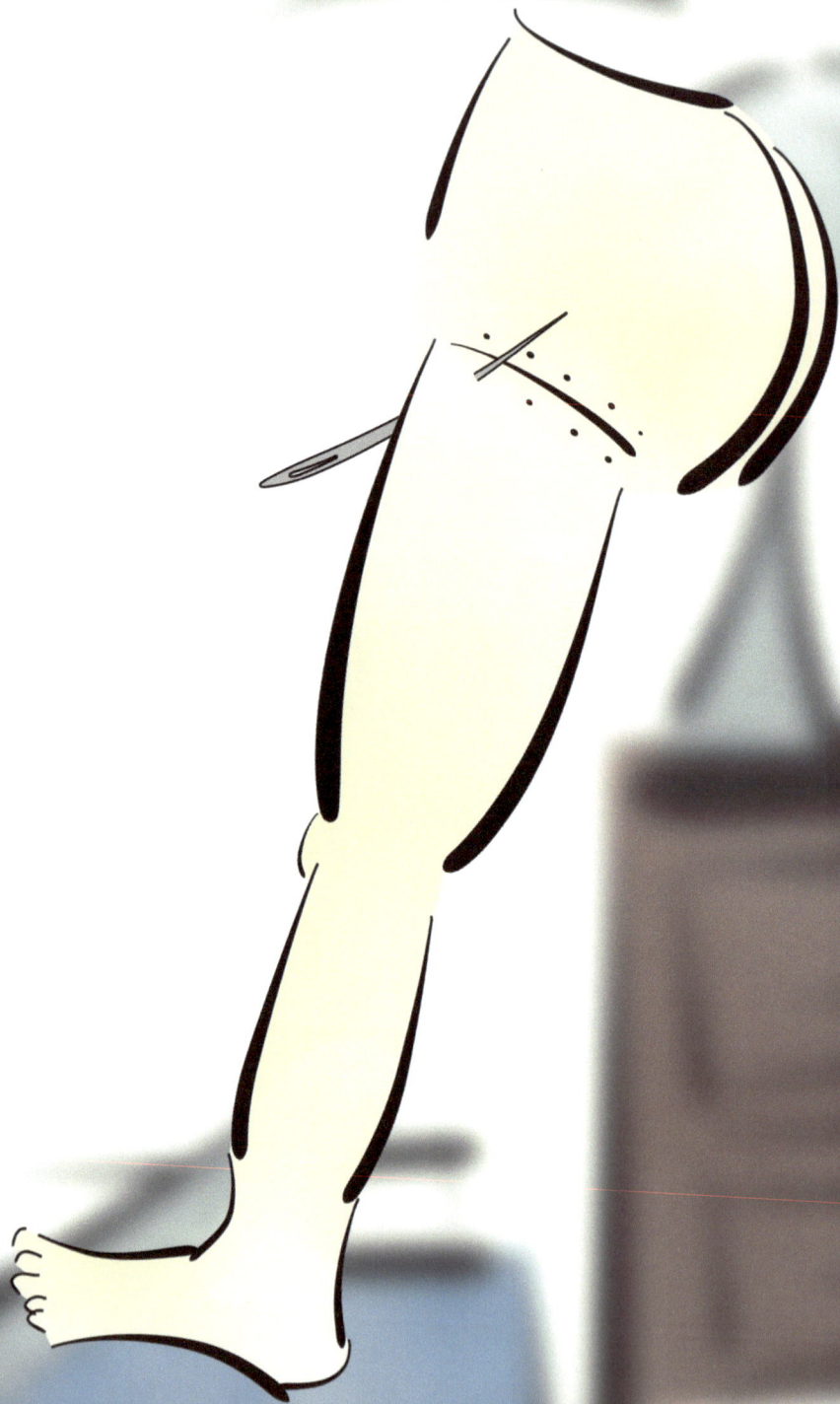

A leg on the butt

Then add his gut and back

Then an arm
and then one more

Oh!
I can only find
his hat and hair

Well
I have a nut
I will just use that

Put on an eye
Then one more
and then a grin

Then a jolt
to make him
come to life

Hey Max
Was that a fart?
Phew!

Yes, oops
And a poop
Yuck!

To mom and dad

As a selfpublisher, user reviews and word-of-mouth are essential to my success. If you liked the book, please review it on www.amazon.com and remember to tell your friends about it on Facebook, Twitter and other social media.

"Max and Mia – Poor Max" is available in both print and e-book formats on Amazon and is available in both Danish and English.

Additionally, my urban fantasy novel "Shades – The Demise of Blake Beck" is also available as e-book and paperback on Amazon (However, this is mainly for the grown-ups).

Apart from books, Widowgrove also makes games – both physical boardgames and digtal games. Find out more about these projects on www.widowgrove.com

- Anders Rauff-Nielsen

Facebook: www.facebook.com/widowgrove
Twitter: @AndersRauff

www.ingramcontent.com/pod-product-compliance
Lightning Source LLC
Chambersburg PA
CBHW041545040426
42447CB00002B/51